TBG Publishing LLC, P.O. Box 861900, Plano, Texas 75086-1900

This publication is designed to provide accurate and authoritative
information in regard to the subject matter covered. It is sold with the
understanding that the publisher is not engaged in rendering professional
services. If professional advice or other expert assistance is required,
the services of a competent professional should be sought.

Library of Congress Control Number: 2009941114

TBG Publishing LLC

            My Friend Just Lost Her Husband:
            The Financial Guide For Moving From Profound Uncertainty
            To Sustained Security / by Dana Barfield.

ISBN 0-977-11321-3

Printed in the United States of America

10 9 8 7 6 5 4 3 2 1

David Oden,

My attorney who clarified the idea…

What people are saying about My Friend Just Lost Her Husband:

"Excellent Advice!" - Lyn B.

"I felt ten feet tall [with this information]!" - Karen B.

"The needed information which you provide would have been so helpful when my sister lost her husband many years ago." - Betty Barrett

"I really like how you address the need and the process [for the widow] to build confidence in her decision-making. You have a great way of helping us non-money minded people understand what is going on." - K Collander

"You taught me how to manage my budget and then you invested my money so I could do more than just survive every month." - Shirley W.

"You provide excellent counsel, along with a genuine concern for the well-being of the widow."

"It is a very comprehensive book on helping widows, not only with finances, but with other aspects of a loss, including helping them work through their emotions." - Beth Way

"This book has a lot of helpful information I never knew and would never think to ask or find out." - Kristin Butler

[This is] "clear, direct, and wise counsel about finding the right individual to care for the financial issues facing the newly widowed woman."

"First it's remarkable that I got connected with you, and second, that you have proven so trustworthy and incredibly effective since I arrived." - Sarah M.

"In his direct and easy-to-comprehend financial guide for women who have lost their husbands, Dana Barfield has provided a resource that could significantly alter the course of the rest of their lives for the better. Wisely directed at the friends of these women, who may be their best allies during those heartrending yet critical first days and months following their loss, Barfield offers practical, step-by-step advice. His professional experience, integrity, and insights into both human character and the grief process make this a unique and trustworthy lifeline in one of life's fiercest storms." - Debbie B.

Acknowledgments

A number of people have contributed to the successful completion of this project.

It is popular these days to "thank the man upstairs" or simply ignore any mention of God at the completion of a job well done. While this is not a religious book per se, all truth originates in some form or fashion, from God's own mouth and from His Word. I consider myself a man created in the image of God, a recipient of remarkable grace through Jesus Christ, as a result a participant in a unique relationship with a holy, yet kind, God, and an aspiring adherent to God's word, the Bible. Based on these realities, everything of value that I know and can use to benefit anyone concerned necessarily comes from Him.

Sherry, Karen, Sarah, Debbie, Joan, Mary Ann, Fran, Judy, Belinda, Wilma, Pam, Shirley, Bev, Sandy, and Brenda were kind enough to share their specific thoughts and experiences. Many other women through out the years have also contributed to the ideas that you will read here.

My friend Carl Panasik had a life changing experience as I was completing this project. It brought a sense of purpose, urgency, and stark reality as something so serious, happened to someone so close. We have been friends for a long time and regularly laugh about the fact that all of the inhabitants of our respective homes are females, with a single, obvious exception at each location. Wanting the best for Debra, Bev, Chelsea, Kristin, Allison, Ryan, and Grandma evokes intense emotion and powerful incentives to wisely provide this service and effectively communicate this information.

Thank you to Kalenda Adams who edited the book. Every comment she made was spot on and delivered in such a way where I knew she had my best interests, and the best interests of my readers, at heart. This book reads far better and is more consistent because of Kalenda. Also to Lois Grotler, whose energy and efforts propelled the project forward.

David Oden is my attorney. It was Oden's brainstorming that prompted me to put this service we have been providing, for what will soon be a quarter century, down on paper.

When I broached the possibility of doing a book on financial guidance for widows, Bob Crowner (MSU) and Dick Gerke (USMC) both said, almost in unison, that they had seen their friend's wives rudderless at the loss of their husbands, that this kind of information was desperately needed, and that I should definitely do the book.

Dr. Richard Hansen was a self described, formerly-aimless boy, whose life was transformed after military service. Growing up in Minnesota in the 50's, no one ever talked to him about college or challenged him to think in those terms. But after serving three years in the Air Force, he attended and subsequently graduated from the University of Minnesota on the G.I. Bill. Over the ensuing years, he developed a much-sought-after, worldwide, expertise in marketing, and effective relationship development/management in the marketing context. Professor saw a need in this book and he very capably addressed it.

Writing a book is hard work. Letting the book out for public viewing is terrifying. My wife Debra read the draft and eased the terror.

Finally, Debra Klawetter www.debraklawetter.com transformed my face into a remarkable back cover photo –

when you see me in person you'll understand what I mean.
Who says there are no more miracles?

My Friend Just Lost Her Husband:

The Financial Guide for Moving from Profound Uncertainty to Sustained Security

By: Dana Barfield

Table of Contents

Prologue

Anything I've ever done that ultimately was
worthwhile, initially scared me to death.
- Betty Bender

Why to the Friend, Instead of the Women?

Every woman I've ever worked with or interviewed, without
exception, has told me, "For the first few weeks I could not
read anything because I was not able to concentrate".
Since she can't concentrate and there is a need to get
accurate and helpful information into "her hands", I'm
writing this book to you, because you care, you can
concentrate, you're needed, and you are in a position to
help and protect your friend.

Why this Resource, Instead of Another?

For more than 23 years I have been advising and assisting
women who have lost their husbands. Men who died in
their 30's, others who died in their 80's, men who died
suddenly from heart attacks, slowly from cancer, at times
that were a complete shock, and at times that were a
complete relief. One woman's husband committed suicide
in the family home leaving her with daunting memories and
twin four year-old sons. I held one man's hand as cancer

took him, and stood at the end of the hospital bed as another simply stopped breathing...

These men have owned businesses, been executives, or tradesman. Some were blue collar, and some white collar. One man worked for Home Depot.

We've sold businesses, worked with attorneys and accountants, dealt with insurance settlements, worked on budgets, negotiated medical expense reductions, worked through real estate issues, and corrected the mistakes of prior poor "advice" – in short, whatever it took to get things on firm footing[1]. This is a welcome, if only, initial relief to the woman who now finds herself without her former companion, confidant, and problem solver[2]. Then **to build an ongoing lifestyle of secure and sustainable income**, we manage investments to reduce risk, keep taxes low, and produce lifetime cash flow so that she knows she (and her young children) are financially protected. We also help

_____

[1] We've also negotiated financial settlements for women going through divorce.
[2] My editor points out that not all women have a great marriage – to which I agree. However, if that marriage was all problems and all difficulties, then she won't be seeing his absence as a loss but instead as liberation and of far lesser difficulty to deal with.

make the necessary adjustments to estate plans, trusts, insurance and tax planning.

In preparation specifically for this book, I took the further step of interviewing a number of other women, who are not our clients. We discovered in those interviews that ***women who do not grieve their loss in healthy ways, make poor financial decisions which compromise or even destroy their financial resources*** (and obviously any sense of security). In response, a section on our observations over the years and the answers we were provided in these interviews about healthy grieving is included. Please know that I am not a trained psychologist. But, equally as true is the fact that one need not be a dairy farmer to recognize a gallon of milk.

Resulting from this experience and these interviews, you'll find the ideas presented here are significant, resonant, and helpful, for they ***have been learned and put into practice in the real world over almost a quarter century***. So as to make maximum use of your thoughtfulness, time, energy, and friendship on behalf of your friend, I don't mince words and I refused to include "fluff". Therefore, I encourage you to read every word carefully.

We've structured the beginning of the book to provide information of background and context that will help you get yourself up to speed quickly about the *changes in attitude and mindset that your friend has gone, and will go, through*. Some of this has nothing explicit or direct to do with financial issues, but fail to understand or address these concerns, and your friend's financial plans are likely to fall quite short of need, much less ideal.

This is because money, while a high priority for your friend, is not her ultimate priority. In order to make wise financial decisions as these are presented to her, *she must have a minimum level of confidence in her decision making ability*. Even if she is deciding on things that in your mind are minor, these are still things that impact her now and long into the future. We have included what is needed to help her get to this point.

As for the financial, benefit, insurance, and tax issues that need to be addressed, we have organized these according to the *time frame and sequence that they need attention*. You'll see sections on what needs to be done in the first week, first month, and first quarter.

There is information and an explanation to help you find the right financial counsel. Based on the issues involved and the requirements attendant to her situation, you should seek qualified professional investment help. This section will *help you to identify who is truly qualified and professional.*

In the back of the book is a convenient list of resources that we have available covering the subjects of social security, taxes, insurance, and other updated relevant subjects. You can access these at our website www.sustainedsecurity.com and www.thebarfieldgroup.com.

Finally, these issues are profoundly important and very personal to your friend, even though at the moment she likely won't articulate this reality. As such, it only makes sense to refer to her by a real name instead of an impersonal pronoun. So instead of "she" or "her" I choose wherever I can to use the name of different women for whom I have great respect for their ability to survive and then thrive in the face of such profound loss. When you read "Sarah" or "Judy" or some other personal name, be reminded that we helped others rebuild sustainable security for themselves under these conditions. With the right assistance and counsel, your friend will do the same.

What are the Benefits of Buying and Reading This Book?

I tell the varnished truth in this book. "Varnish" is a clear liquid designed to protect wood without changing any of the substance or appearance characteristics of wood. This book is designed to communicate facts and information that protect your friend, enable you both to see issues clearly and accurately, and propel her forward to reestablishing her personal and financial security.

Belinda (personal instead of impersonal pronoun), and every other woman I have interviewed and/or worked for, possesses an inborn and innate desire for security. Losing her husband puts her in a position of profound uncertainty. Belinda's reality is now different, her decision making process has changed, her response to changing circumstances has been altered, and as a result her confidence is shaken. Even if she has "plenty of money" there is uncertainty about managing it, investing it, matching cash flow with expenses, and making it last. All of these elements must be addressed and the foundations rebuilt for Belinda to be and feel secure.

Specifically Belinda must get to the place where she:
- Sees reality accurately and accepts it,

- Possesses the ability to respond successfully to changing circumstances,
- Assembles relevant information, accurately evaluates it, and makes wise decisions,
- Experiences her situation truly improving based on her response and decision making, and
- Is able to meet her financial needs through work and/or investment.

Giving you the tools and information needed to help Belinda work through her fear and accomplish these five objectives is the purpose and the benefit of this book.

Chapter 1 - The Right Person for the Job

To the world you may be just one person, but to one person you may be the world. An adventure is only an inconvenience rightly considered. An inconvenience is an adventure wrongly considered.
--G. K. Chesterton

We're talking about the most serious and important situation in Ann's life. At this point, all of her financial "mulligans" are over (if she truly ever had any to begin with). Decisions must be right the first time. She must be protected from people with conflicted interests, lack of experience, ignorance, and/or outright fraud, who would claim to "advise" her. She must get her finances settled and in order, all while structuring them to provide adequate income for the rest of her life.

As Ann's friend, you are being asked at this critical stage to 1) Evaluate your relationship and ability to help her, and then, 2) Commit to assisting Ann in this difficult and profoundly important time in her life. These are serious matters requiring thoughtful consideration on your part. Two things are essential here: If you discover that you are not the right person for this role and responsibility, you must refuse it. But, if on careful (albeit swift) examination it becomes clear that you share the kind of relationship necessary to help Ann, it is equally imperative that you step up. You are being called to assist someone who profoundly needs you.

Use the rest of this chapter to evaluate yourself and your relationship with Ann. Understand no relationship will demonstrate all of these characteristics perfectly. But every significant relationship will have many of these as a foundation.

- Whether or not you are a relative of Ann's is irrelevant. Don't assume that just because you are a relative that you are the correct person for the job. On the other hand, don't let your role in the family, or lack of blood relationship, preclude you either. This simply does not matter.

- This friend could be a man or a woman. Some women are more comfortable with a man; some with a woman. Whichever the case may be is only relevant in one situation: Ann is sad, lonely, and vulnerable. She has lost her partner. If you are a man, you must avoid even the slightest hint of sexual overtone or activity. She is not ready for this, even if she says she is. It will confuse her, compromise your integrity (at a minimum), and cloud the judgment and decision making ability for both of you. If there is even the slightest possibility of this problem surfacing, you must excuse yourself now. If you believe that you will have no problem here, please proceed, but bear clearly in mind that protective men have a soft spot for hurting women (and vice versa), and you are being asked to provide protection at a meaningful level. My strong recommendation is that you exhibit wise discretion by communicating to another person (I rely on my wife in this role) an ongoing general overview of what you are doing. It is essential to maintain Ann's confidentiality, however you can still make yourself accountable without communicating or compromising details of her life and financial situation. I tell my wife with whom I am meeting, the general subject matter, where the meeting is occurring, and how long it will take. On top of that, I have my wife, my assistant, or someone else in the office with me while the meeting is taking place.

- You and Ann will have exchanged conversation and ideas on a substantial level. This may not have occurred daily, weekly, or even monthly, but when you have talked, it was about relevant, meaningful, and important matters. You are someone who gets (and gives) an honest answer from Ann when you ask, "What's going on?"

- Your motives must be Ann's best interests ahead of yours. Maintain your own family and responsibilities – your life there continues, but your own interests of new business, an enhanced reputation, or improved social standing must be set aside now. This is you, coming to Ann's aid simply because Ann needs this from you and no other reason. You must have as the priority, a genuine sense of concern for her wellbeing and cannot have any conflicts between her interests and your own.

- You must be able to identify and preempt from getting to Ann, those who lack sound judgment or have ulterior motives.

- You must have a willingness to graciously, but firmly ask relevant questions of Ann and others, even when these are difficult. What I mean by graciously in this and the following cases, is primarily a concern for Ann's thoughts and feelings. This is the question you'll need to constantly ask yourself: What needs to be done for Ann, in her best interests, while respecting her concerns on the matter? Know that Ann's mindset is but one consideration, because Ann's thinking is going to be scrambled to some degree. This is where the ability to have Ann's best interests at heart come to the forefront, because what she wants, thinks, or feels may not be in her best interest, and you must be able to come to the right conclusions, leading her to the correct decisions, given all the relevant factors.

- You need to be able to tell the truth graciously. Some people are always nice. Some people tell the truth even if it hurts other people's feelings. You'll need to do both. Most people will back off if they receive kind, but firm communication. But some won't. In the event someone just can't get the message or if something proposed for her is simply not beneficial, you must be able to say (or help her to say), "No! I'm sorry, but the answer is NO."

- You should be able to "put yourself in her shoes". It is tremendously helpful if you can arrive at accurate information or appropriate decisions relative to Ann by asking yourself, "If this happened to me, what would I want done?"

- You have the ability to see situations accurately and graciously move them forward. This is to include situations that could involve Ann's children, relatives, living arrangements, relationships, activities, finances, and/or legal matters.

- It is helpful if you have experienced a profound loss and successfully grieved through it.

- You know enough about Ann's life to have a sense of who gets access to Ann and who does not. You understand how to screen and communicate from people to Ann and from Ann to other people.

- You can answer the call that comes to Ann's house asking, "What can I do?" without having to ask Ann what needs to be done.

- You have the ability to help propel Ann forward, helping her make progress in rebuilding her life, without you taking over or Ann handing over her life. Your objective is to work yourself out of a job where she is dependent on her own resources, instead of into a situation where she is forever dependent upon you. Initially, her dependence upon you will be high and that is why you are being called into this situation. But, the best, kindest, and most beneficial thing you can do for Ann is to graciously transition her off of dependence on you and onto herself.

If you have a caring, sharing relationship of mutual respect with Ann, you must now step up. Now is the time for you to take initiative to come to Ann's side to aid and protect her. You are needed so that Ann avoids all kinds of personal and financial perils that can compromise and damage her, potentially for the rest of her life.

Chapter 2 - New State of Mind

"Nine requisites for contented living:
Health enough to make work a pleasure.
Wealth enough to support your needs.
Strength to battle with difficulties and
overcome them.
Grace enough to confess your sins and
forsake them.
Patience enough to toil until some good is
accomplished.
Charity enough to see some good in your
neighbor.
Love enough to move you to be useful and
helpful to others.
Faith enough to make real the things of
God.
Hope enough to remove all anxious fears
concerning the future."

--Johann Wolfgang von Goethe

After something so difficult as losing her husband, Sarah's thinking will be affected. It does not matter whether his end was a surprise or expected, peaceful or violent, sudden or over some period of time. Here are some unanimously common things that you can expect Sarah to now think, feel, and/or experience.

Think through these issues in advance. It may be that she will express them to you on her own and you will now understand what she is talking about. It could be that she senses these things, but feels frustration at not being able to articulate them – you'll be able to assist in leading her to say what she is thinking and experiencing, thus reducing her frustration. It could be that none of this will consciously register in her mind until months or years later. In this case, you'll at least have a framework to understand what she does say, and why she does certain things that are different from the way she previously handled them.

• Regardless of the relationship Sarah had with her husband, in almost all but the rarest of cases, this is the most difficult thing she will ever deal with. Doesn't matter if they were married five years or fifty.

• Sarah has an immediate and profound understanding that everything in her life has now changed – "radically" is the word I hear most frequently. Regardless of her family situation this is reality, but if Sarah has small children, it is even more drastic. Many women describe this as having a sense that they have just "gone over a cliff", in which they "don't know what is at the bottom, but [they] do know it won't be pretty". While on the surface this appears to be a very negative and pessimistic statement, don't be too troubled by it. For most women this is very healthy, as it helps her begin the process of accepting and adapting to reality – or in other words, grieve in a healthy way.

- The complete uncertainty of what is "at the bottom" and the concern "that it won't be pretty" creates anxiety for Sarah. She doesn't really know what's coming, she thinks it will be ugly when it arrives, and she worries. Let's face it, this will be extremely hard. You will lose credibility with her if you tell her, "Don't worry dear, everything will work out perfectly" or "This is obviously God's will for you…". What I say to all the women I counsel is this, and you should memorize these words so that you can say them AND MEAN THEM. "No matter what happens, we will work through this together." At this time in her life, the honest response, rather than the eternally optimistic one works far, far better in dealing with her anxiety and building trust for her.

- Initially Sarah will not feel like eating and she probably won't be able to sleep. She may want to stay with you or have you stay with her for a couple days. This is very accurately portrayed in the movie "The Pelican Brief", where after the death of her boyfriend, Julia Robert's character Darby Shaw musters all the strength she has to ask Denzel Washington's character

Greg Grantham, "Would you mind sleeping on the sofa (in the other room)?" She just did not want to stay alone at a time when she felt so vulnerable. Greg Grantham in the next room allowed her to finally get a good night's rest and you can see in the subsequent (and accurate) scenes in the movie that she started to be a little more energetic and productive.

- After a couple days Sarah will want to go home to be back in familiar surroundings, where she can be the most comfortable. Do not be alarmed when she is not what you previously knew as "comfortable", but take her at face value when she says she's "most comfortable at home". Several women suggested that after an initial period of shock and sleeplessness usually lasting three to four nights, they learned to schedule very active days, so that at the end of the day, they were too tired not to sleep.

- The thought of food may make Sarah nauseous. If she has children, you can help by making certain they: get some food that they will eat, bathed, clean/pressed clothes, teeth brushed and in bed as normally as possible. We'll say more about this later, but realize that Sarah's children will have questions about what has happened. Sarah should be the one to answer their questions tactfully but truthfully. This helps her begin the grieving process in healthy and productive ways.

- As I mentioned in the first words of this book, Sarah will have an inability to focus (on anything) for more than a minute or two. This makes reading, managing finances, accumulating information necessary for decision making, decision making itself, housework, office work, and potentially driving, very difficult, if not impossible. She may, or may not, have a heightened sense of awareness for her children. She won't be able to concentrate for probably a couple weeks. Most women say they could not read for six to twelve months afterward.

- There is an immediate "altered state" that Sarah will enter into. Some women describe this as "numbness". Others recount it to be far more like a "fog" rather than "numbness", because they feel the pain of the loss of their husband. They go on to say that when one can feel this profound pain, numbness cannot be the case. Imagine yourself driving at night in a dense fog. This is unsettling and creates tremendous uncertainty. Who's in front of me? What if they stop suddenly? Who's behind me? What if I stop suddenly? Where is the side of the road? Is there oncoming traffic? Now just imagine driving in this fog with a migraine headache. This is very close to how Sarah feels. If she describes it either way (numbness or fog), now you can understand what she is talking about. If she struggles to say what she is experiencing, rather than telling her what it is, ask her, "Do you feel numb?" or "Do things seem foggy to you?" These gentle questions may open up Sarah's ability to now talk about things she is struggling to identify.

*   Numbness (or the fog) is not the same thing as dumbness! Do not mistake the extra time Sarah now takes, or the uncertainty she communicates as newfound ignorance. She is still very smart and still very capable, she simply is experiencing, albeit on a bigger scale, the same responses and feelings that come from a Novocain shot at the dentist or a car trip in late night fog. Do not be alarmed or surprised that her response times are slower - some out of necessity and some out of fear/confusion.

*   Sarah, regardless of how diligent and disciplined she was before, will experience a sense of "paralysis". She knows that she is in a situation that weighs heavy on her. She may see this as intense pressure. She

knows that there are decisions that she needs to make. She probably has the sense that her entire future rests on these decisions, but she does not know what to do. I encourage you not to make her decisions for her. **I strongly encourage you NOT to make her decisions for her.** What you can do is assemble the information needed for her to make the decision. Boil it down to a summary on one sheet of paper. Walk her through the information while having the longer supporting documents available in which to refer. If a decision needs to be made in two days, do not wait until the last minute to provide the summary information. Walk her through the summary 24-48 hours before she has to decide, then walk her through it again when the time comes to decide, then ask her for HER decision. This does more to propel Sarah forward in a healthy way, than most anything else you can do for her. You will be tempted to simply make her decisions – it's faster, it's easier. But it also extends her period of grief, fog, and paralysis. Lead her firmly, but gently through the process of making her own decisions and it will be the most loving gift you could ever give to her.

- Sarah's previous ways of relaxing and relieving pressure are unlikely to work because she can't concentrate. Reading is impossible. Hand work such as sewing, cross stitch, embroidery, and quilting are probably out. She may be too tired to exercise. One suggestion is Netflix or something similar, but let her choose the movies. Giving her a choice that has so little risk or downside is a great way to jump start her decision making.

- Everyone I have ever talked to, regardless of religious affiliation, relationship, or persuasion said they felt tremendous disappointment and/or anger with God over their loss. Sarah will feel this way at some point if she is properly grieving. Do not condemn her for these feelings of anger, but do not assuage them either. Encourage her to tell God herself how she feels in the best way she knows how. Whatever Sarah says to Him, He can handle. Allowing and encouraging her, when she senses these feelings, to honestly express her deepest emotions to God is vitally important for her. It is one of the most, if not the most healthy thing that she can do.

Chapter 3 - Good Grief

No one can go back and make a brand new
start, my friend, but anyone can start from
here and make a brand new end.
- Dan Zadra

As I write this, most, if not every country on the planet is
working through the worst economic conditions since the
Depression of the 1930's. Unemployment is high.
Businesses are struggling. Homes are hard to buy
because of the lack of mortgage financing. Tax increases
are being considered. State and municipal governments
are cutting budgets because of significant deficits.
Individuals and families are afraid to spend any money.

This entire mess occurred because mortgage borrowers,
mortgage lenders, banks, investment houses, and
investors all "took a vacation" from reality. Borrowers took
out loans they had no way of repaying, lenders loaned
money they knew would not be repaid, banks and
investment houses abandoned common sense by ignoring
the possibility that the price of a house could go down.
Ultimately, by using complex, but deeply flawed
mathematical models, investors in these mortgages

convinced themselves that "they didn't have any risk at all"![3] Counselors call this mindset "denial".

What does all this have to do with grieving? Grieving is the slow process of embracing reality; it is Mary, over time, coming to full and accurate acceptance of the terrible loss she has experienced in her husband's death. This is extremely important! The entire world economic meltdown could have been avoided if people stayed grounded in reality. What sane man would borrow money he cannot repay?? What intelligent woman would loan money she knew wouldn't be repaid? How could anyone come to the conclusion that there is no risk to investing? The answer is only someone who was ignoring reality, someone who was in denial!

Healthy, appropriately processed grief brings Mary back to reality. Grounded in reality, she can and will make good decisions. In the coming months and years Mary will be called on to make many decisions, some of great significance, and being grounded in reality will be crucial. When she can take information and make sound decisions with it, she experiences an increased sense of security. With the accurate sense of security comes better decision

---

[3] Recipe for Disaster: The Formula That Killed Wall Street, Felix Salmon, Wired magazine 2/23/2009

making, with better decision making comes more security, and so on.

Steps in the Process of Healthy Grieving

There are five widely acknowledged steps in the grieving process – the process of embracing reality.

Stage 1 – "I cannot believe this happened!"
Stage 2 – "I'm angry that this happened!"
Stage 3 – "What did I do to cause this to happen?!"
Stage 4 – "I'm devastated by what happened!"
Stage 5 – "I accept that this happened."

When you hear Mary make these statements or ask this kind of question, it is a sign that she is making progress; that she is moving in a healthy direction. *When she talks like this, encourage her to continue. Ask her what she means, to explain her thinking, or to tell you more, ask how she came to this conclusion, and above all do NOT inhibit or scold her for these statements!*

How Long Will This Take?

The process of grieving is very much like the process of forgiveness. When someone hurts us badly, we can hold that against the person forever or we can choose not to seek revenge and not to repay them "evil for evil". In the first few days after the incident, we are frequently tempted to get back at them. In these early stages, forgiveness requires that each time we remember the hurt and are tempted, we decide not to seek revenge. As time passes, the remembrances and temptations are fewer and farther between. But still some event or encounter several years after the trouble may bring the hurt to the surface. When this happens we reaffirm the decision not to repay or seek revenge.

Mary's healthy grieving will be very much like this process of forgiveness. Her emotions will be raw in the beginning as she can't think of anything but her tremendous loss. She will experience serious bouts of denial, anger, absence of any hope whatsoever, and blame herself for the loss. As time passes and she begins to embrace reality, these emotions will decrease in frequency, but will likely never completely subside. Each time one pops up, she will need to reaffirm her decision to embrace what happened and accept reality.

In order for Mary to initially move through the steps of grieving, she must answer each of her statements/questions for herself. You cannot do it for her.

You should not rush her. The best things you can do for her are listen and encourage her to talk through it by drawing out her thoughts.

In many cases, she may move through the stages without much prodding from you. She may take more time at one stage than another. Mary will move through stage 1 when she acknowledges and reconciles in her own mind that her husband really did die. She'll move through stage 2 sometime around her being able to say, "You know, I'm really mad about this!" Stage 3 will come when she can say, "His death was not my fault". She moves through stage 4 when she can express optimism and see opportunity again in life. Just like the process of forgiveness, don't be alarmed if she works back through the stages at various times.

Denial Ain't Just a River in Egypt

The opposite of healthy grieving is denial. Denial is the ongoing refusal or inability to think about and accept the reality of the situation. Remember that the first step of grieving is denial. Initial denial is healthy – ongoing denial leads to meltdown in one form or another. Remain calm at the initial expression of denial as this is healthy. But, if six months have gone by and it is clear Mary is still in denial, this is cause for concern.

Denial occurs because Mary thinks her situation is all encompassing – she recognizes no solution and no person who is bigger than her problem(s). If you've ever been exposed to Alcoholics Anonymous, you know that one of the early steps of working to sobriety is to "acknowledge a higher power". The existence of a higher power enables Mary to see someone "bigger" than her troubles; someone of ability and willingness who can enable her to work successfully through them. Mary, and for that matter you, may not be "religious". Every woman we have ever worked with or interviewed, regardless of religious persuasion has, after some period of time, acknowledged "that it is clear God has looked out for me – this has not been easy, but it could have been much worse than it was."

The Jewish Torah and the Christian Bible say that "In the beginning, God created the heavens and the earth". This is a very comforting statement if you think about it. For since God created everything that we have, He, by definition and simple logic, must be bigger than the problems we have. Since this is the reality of God, Mary can call on and rely on Him to help her.

Everyone Responds a Little Differently

Each woman has her own unique personality, therefore each woman responds to situations differently. Psychologists have identified four basic personality types so as to suggest helpful ways of communicating and interacting with different people. Well-known counselor, Dr. John Trent popularized the use of different animal personalities[4] to make it easy to remember the basic differences between people.

First is the Otter. An otter is a free wheeling, fun loving, pool party waiting to happen. The otter is always seeking to <u>have fun</u>.

Second, is the Golden Retriever. No animal is more <u>loyal</u> or more faithful than a Golden Retriever. The Golden Retriever is seeking the good old days.

There is the Beaver. The beaver works constantly and with <u>diligence</u>, regardless of circumstances, always

---

[4] Dr. John Trent gave me permission to use his personality descriptions that have been based on four animals. They can give meaningful insight into the different ways people grieve. You can learn more about these personalities in his book, The Two Sides of Love, available at his website www.strongfamilies.com.

accomplishing huge tasks, one small bite at a time. The beaver is seeking a pattern.

Finally, the Lion. This animal is the <u>leader</u> acting firmly and decisively to move forward while identifying and protecting against danger. The lion is seeking resolution and success.

As you read through the list of the creatures and envision for yourself their personalities, which one most closely relates to your "Mary"? In the following pages, we'll work through the mindset, grief process, decision making process, challenges, and how you can approach and help your friend deal with her grief in a healthy way, consistent with her basic personality type.

Remember, that the personality and character strengths Mary possesses, which seem to be weaknesses in dealing with grief, are actually the strengths and traits she needs to have appealed to and employ to make progress in grieving. She is going to deal with this and every other situation she has/encounters according to her basic personality. The following descriptions will help you know how to lead her as you encounter challenges together.

After you have located and studied Mary's personality type and how to assist her accordingly, make sure that you go to the end of this chapter and read **Additional Thoughts on Grieving** where more ideas given for helping Mary regardless of her personality type. **This final part of this chapter is extremely important!**

The Otter

Otter's Mindset:

- How can we have fun?
- How can we avoid discomfort?
- Let's deal with this problem later.
- What responsibility?
- Focus, schmocus!

Otter's Grief Process

- Her grieving appears to be no trouble whatsoever early on because she ignores pain.
- She appears to be dealing remarkably well with her pain, likely because she is ignoring it.
- She will probably move to the fun aspects of her new reality pretty readily.

- She may re-engage in dating much sooner than people around her think is appropriate.
- She has the ability to (apparently) ignore pain for a really long time – but it eventually catches up with her.
- Simple grief issues can take her years to come to terms with, because she wants to avoid them.

Otter's Decision Making Process

- Frequently her decision making process is to have someone else decide. She may demonstrate this by asking you to decide for her, or simply making no decision and letting consequences play out – this can create havoc in her bill paying, insurance settlements, estate issues, and credit.
- She will decide to take the route with the least trouble and/or the most fun – which frequently may not be the correct route.
- She may say things like, "I know that I need to decide, but I can't", "you decide for me", "I don't want to think about that", or "when is the last possible time that I can make this decision?"

Otter's Challenges

- Making decisions.

- Working through anything painful.
- Expressing anger and subsequently moving through the remaining grief stages.
- She tends to get stuck in grief stage 1 – denial – "I can't believe this happened", even though it appears by her smiling face and happy demeanor that she has worked completely through her grief – this is likely a form of denial.
- She generally won't ask for help, but when sincere help is offered, she is likely to accept it. This is partly so she doesn't have to deal with the "pain".
- The otter has the most challenging personality to come to terms with pain.

How you can Approach and Help the Otter

- Everyone is going to really be confronted by the pain of their loss sometime during their lifetime. The longer that the otter waits, the worse it will be. At the same time you cannot force her to deal with the reality of her pain. Since she trends toward fun to begin with, you may be able to help her make progress in grieving by asking her to talk about fun times she had with her late husband, and after some period of time, asking what fun things she plans to do in the future.

- You likely won't be able to reach her by saying, "You need to grieve now, because if you don't, it will be worse later." She has made a lifetime habit of avoiding future pain by having fun now, and this will not move her one inch in that direction.

- After a couple weeks ask her if she feels angry. She will likely say no. Follow up with, "How could you not be angry when someone you had so much fun with has been taken from you?" Give her time (perhaps a few hours to a few weeks) to think about this statement. If she expresses anger over her loss during this period, you're making progress.

- After she expresses anger, ask her if she feels guilty about her husband's death. In all likelihood, with her personality type, she does feel guilty. Over the course of a couple weeks, have her tell you what she feels guilty about.

- After she expresses guilt (again over as much as a couple weeks time) ask what she hopes to do in the future. If you get a glib or flippant answer, ask her how she could possibly be hopeful when she has lost the person that she had so much fun with in the past? Does she really think that those kinds of relationships happen all the time?!

- If she will answer your questions sincerely over a period of weeks or a few months, you have helped her through the initial grief processing period.

The Golden Retriever

Golden Retriever's Mindset

- Finds it disloyal and as a result very difficult to move forward.
- My life will never be the same!
- My pain will never go away!
- Let's deal with this eternally!
- Let's focus on what was lost.

Golden Retriever's Grief Process

- She will focus on what "used to be".
- She will say her life will never be the same, but mean it will never, ever be as good.
- She will be very reluctant to engage in or embrace new activities.
- She is likely to express deep emotions and cry quite frequently over her loss.

- The pet Golden Retriever always seems to be smiling graciously, regardless of circumstances, and she may put on this front also.
- She may appear to deal very poorly with the situation because of emotion and crying – which actually is good, or she may appear to not have a care in the world – which is not good.
- She will tend to get stuck in the fourth stage of grief – I am devastated.
- She may completely skip the first three stages and go directly to I am devastated.
- She will be reluctant to try new things or meet new people.

Golden Retriever's Decision Making Process

- I can't decide!
- I know I need to decide, but I don't know what to do.
- What would [her former husband] do in this situation?
- She may even get to the place where she thinks, "What's the use in deciding?!"

Golden Retriever's Challenges

- It will likely be a challenge for this woman to move on with her life.

- She may tend to grieve and feel very blue for longer than desirable.
- She will likely find it difficult to see new opportunities or feel optimistic about anything. She is likely to feel disloyal to her deceased husband if she tries something new without him.
- Because she feels pessimistic, when she finally does make decisions, she may rush ahead instead of thinking them through clearly.

How you can Approach and Help the Golden Retriever

- Frequently you can help the Golden Retriever by asking her "what would your husband want you to do in this case?" She responds to this because of her sense of loyalty to him.
- It is important afterward to reinforce for her, that even though she considered what he would have done in the same situation, it was still her decision and she made a good one. Several of these situations are likely to help her begin to gain some equilibrium in her grieving.
- Realize that if you try to move too fast to new things, she will resist to the point of shutting down. Better to help her see past progress as a means to evaluating new things, than to push too quickly.

- She gains confidence as she sees she has made good decisions – even small ones – which are the best place for her to start.

The Beaver

Beaver's Mindset

- Disciplined and efficient
- Seeks a pattern or a system of bite-sized steps to address challenges and opportunities
- Analytical
- A place for everything and everything in its place
- She is likely to see challenges as problems to be solved.
- I wish I could get someone to help me, but no one can do it as well as I can do it myself.
- It takes more time to teach someone to do it, than it just takes me to do it myself.
- There is nothing that I can do about what has already happened, so let's focus on the task at hand.

Beaver's Grief Process

- How can I get things back to normal?

- What must I do to restore peace and order?
- What pain? I don't feel any pain – there's work to be done!
- You ask me why I'm not dealing with "this"? There is nothing to deal with – I have things to do.
- Just like the animal beaver who works relentlessly regardless of weather or other challenges, she is likely to simply refuse to hurt.
- She probably won't cry or show much emotion in front of others.
- She will appear to be calm, collected, and making progress on things.

Beaver's Decision Making Process

- What is the logical decision?
- What do the numbers say?
- I'll work through my analysis and then I will decide.

Beaver's Challenges

- She may struggle to acknowledge her pain to herself, much less anyone else.
- She can get stuck in grief stage 2 – anger, because the loss of her husband upset the carefully crafted system she had created to deal with life. While they can get

stuck here, you are not likely to see outward manifestations of anger – beavers are too under control to let that happen.

- When you hear the stories these days of people who went in and shot up their co-workers, or a church, you frequently hear: "This was a quiet person, always did his work well, never really made any trouble for anyone, I just can't believe that he would do this..." – clearly the beaver personality. Beavers work and they ignore any pain to "get their work done". But failing to deal with pain doesn't make pain go away. Instead, denial intensifies pain which ultimately works its way out in other very destructive ways.
- She is unlikely to ask for help. "I can do it myself"!
- She probably needs assistance building joy into her life.
- She needs help recognizing, understanding, and expressing her emotions in any way, and even more so in a healthy way.

How you can Approach and Help the Beaver

- Remembering that she very much likes order and a system, ask how you can be helpful in her system. Ask her to make a list of the steps that she wants you to follow.

- Ask her what steps her husband would have taken or recommended to deal with the problem.
- Show her the stages in the grieving process; Ask her where she currently sees herself <u>and why</u>. Ask her what steps are needed for her to get to the next stage.
- She will likely have no trouble getting to stage 2, because her system or process was interrupted and she'll be angry about it (though she won't be out of control). To get her thinking in terms of stage 3, ask her if her system ever got in the way of appreciating her husband, did her system ever interfere with fun they could have had together, did her husband ever suggest that she "stop and smell the roses"? What did she think about that then? What does she think about it now? Let her mull this over for up to several weeks.
- To get to stage 4 ask her where the system is coming apart with her husband gone. Where is she struggling to get things back in order? What parts of her system simply no longer work? Again let her consider this for a couple weeks.
- If and when she gets to the point where she admits she is devastated, ask her how she plans modifying her days and activities to accommodate the changes now that her husband is gone.
- After she has processed through these questions over a couple months, invite her to "bring her system" to a

new group or committee that needs to be better administered or organized.

The Lion

Lion's Mindset

- What is best?
- Where are we right now? Where do we want to go? How do we get there?
- Let's not worry about trouble right now – we'll deal with it when it comes up.
- Let's focus on what is before us.

Lion's Grief Process

- She will not let pain interfere with meeting the needs of those around her.
- After a completed project and in the down time before the next one, she is likely to sense her pain and loss.
- She will likely show concern for others before herself.
- She is likely to struggle over looking out for herself in even the smallest issues until everyone else has been comforted and had their needs met.

Lion's Decision Making Process

- What's the best decision considering all known factors?
- She will consider both the numbers in an issue and the things that cannot be quantified, to arrive at the best possible decision.
- If she is very young or completely surprised by her husband's death, she may make decisions too quickly.
- She will intuitively understand when a decision must be made and she will make it.

Lion's Challenges

- She is likely to say, "I'll grieve later, but I don't have time to worry about that now."
- She may try and take on too much responsibility in this new situation.
- If you demand that she do things according to someone else's code, you will be cut off.
- If you hastily or without knowing all of the facts, criticize her decisions, you will be cut off.
- If you presume upon her, you will be cut off.

How you can Approach and Help the Lion

- Do not flatter her falsely.
- Do not criticize her.

- She is likely to need rest, but feel like she can't spare the time. See if you can schedule coffee, brunch, or lunch with her.
- She may need perspective over the possibility that she is trying to do too much. Ask her if there is anything that she can delegate to you or others?
- She is probably seeking to live up to someone's expectations in all this – her mom or dad, her deceased husband's – someone. Affirm for her what she is truly doing well, but do not offer false praise.
- When she does disclose something, **listen only and do not offer advice**. When she wants advice, she is confident enough to ask for it. Otherwise, just listen to her, because by talking she is processing through things.
- If she does ask, you must give advice that is well reasoned and thought out. If you are not prepared or do not know, tell her that you're not prepared or that you do not know, but that you will do your homework and get back to her promptly. Then do just that.
- Ask her what you can do to be of assistance.
- Observe what is taking place in her life. Make a specific offer that fits a need you observe. If she consents, accomplish that need for her without drama or fanfare.

- If she gets stuck in the stages of grieving, ask her about it, and let her talk.
- If she simply refuses to deal with her grief, say something like, "Mary, as observant and intelligent as you are, you've seen others who overlooked the inevitable in their marriages, with their kids, or at work to their own serious detriment – too many people are depending upon you for you to let that happen here. *Please*, tell me how you're really doing."

Additional Thoughts on Grieving

Spend some time studying the different aspects of the four basic personalities. Mary needs you more than ever at this point in her life. You've got to be able to recognize the ways that she communicates in order to provide the help she needs. Women are frequently surprised to learn just how much of the communication that Mary gives is unspoken by her or not consciously known to her. Understanding and responding properly to her basic personality will make you far more useful and effective in helping Mary build security back into her life.

The person who fares the best in grieving is the one who will accept the short term pain, for the pain is dissipated as it is worked through. If it is never worked through, or if the natural process of working through it is delayed, it seems that there is no pain. The opposite is actually true. The longer Mary puts off dealing with her loss, the worse it will be. Shorter term pain produces longer term benefits.

If Mary has small children she is likely to grieve in very healthy and timely ways – she has little choice because her kids are asking her all the "grieving" questions. If a neighbor or friend's child approaches Mary with questions about "what happened to your husband", or "why are you so sad Aunt Mary?" your tendency will be to protect Mary by whisking the child away or chastising the kid for asking such a "rude" question. That's the worst thing you can do. A child asking Mary what happened gives her an opportunity to deal with reality in a very tender-hearted fashion. What's more, the child will listen, won't offer advice, will share Mary's concern, and then love on Mary. That's exactly what Mary needs – to be invited to talk honestly and tenderly, be listened to, understood, and appropriately loved on.

Regardless of personality type, encourage Mary to eat wisely and get regular exercise. These are easy ways for you to help. Make lunch and invite her over. Ask her to go for a walk through the neighborhood. This kind of thing provides an excellent opportunity for you to assist in the ways we've discussed in this chapter.

Be aware that a woman who is "others centered" may struggle with her own grieving.

If Mary is a person with a very rosy outlook on life, she may have the most difficult time coming to terms with reality. Be aware in this situation that her actions and appearances may be a conscious or unconscious attempt to mask her pain. Putting on a "happy" face will blow up and cause later decisions and problems that are most regrettable.

Help Mary be mindful of the fact that other people who are in denial about death will say incredibly silly, trite, or stupid things. Help her not to be surprised or overly upset about this by providing her with this perspective. Remind her that someone in denial cannot really be expected to be helpful or intelligent, regardless of how well intentioned they are, because those who deny are not dealing in reality themselves. If they're denying reality, there is no way they can be of real help.

Also, be aware that some people, though truly well-intentioned, just have poor social skills under pressure; that some people have never been through this, they genuinely

care, and just don't know what to say; and finally, that
some people are just flat out wrong.

Chapter 4 - Avoiding a Horror Story

"Often regret is very false and displaced, and imagines the past to be totally other than it was."
- John O'Donohue

When I write this chapter I am speaking from what I have witnessed personally or what has been told to me directly. Everything you are about to read is absolutely real, except for the identifying details.

Housewife Horror

I was told this one by the woman's adult child. A woman in her sixties lost her husband after an illness that lasted about a year. As a couple, they were able to comfort one another, prepare for his passing, get their affairs in order, and get as ready as possible for what happened. They had been married to each other their entire adult life, raised several very productive and honorable members of society, and had never strayed from one another during their marriage. He had a lucrative career and had amassed, what can only be described as a considerable nest egg, which was more than adequate to provide. They had a summer home and a winter home within wonderful communities of friendships.

After the husband's passing, Jane apparently began to think she was missing something in life – perhaps that her life had been boring. She met a golf pro. She sold the summer home. The golf pro, who had no money himself, wanted her to get a home in another area close to his golf course. She sold the winter home she had, left her community of friends, and bought another home an hour away in the heat of the real estate market, so she could be with the "exciting love of her life". Over the months she realized, in polite terms, that her golf pro didn't have her best interests in mind. She threw him out. However, the real estate market had collapsed. Now she is stuck with a home, away from her friends, valued at a fraction of what she bought it for, and even though she has significant real estate connections, the house can't be sold and she no longer can afford the mortgage. All of her investments are compromised. Jane will likely have to go to work. This horror occurred because of an artificial perception that her life was boring.

New Best Friend Horror

I witnessed this one. The mother of a single woman died under "normal" circumstances. Sheila's mom left her several hundred thousand dollars in an inheritance. Sheila, in her mid-forties, had little experience with money other than to budget her regular paycheck. She knew nothing about how to deal with complex taxes, how, into what, and when to invest, nor whom she could trust to help her with this kind of work.

An acquaintance she had known casually for some time was a "mutual fund expert". Instantly, this person became Sheila's "best friend", promising to "handle" whatever was needed to get Sheila's money properly invested. The "best friend" sold Sheila a coin collection worth $.25 on the dollar. Even though she had no training as a lawyer or license to practice law, she "drafted" a will and trust (by copying a fill-in-the-blank boiler plate document) naming herself as trustee and beneficiary of everything, in the event something happened to Sheila. She invested other money in expensive insurance products and mutual funds.

Slowly statements began to come in and Sheila realized her "best friend" had caused her mother's assets to dwindle to less than a third of what Sheila had originally received. This horror occurs because people come out of the wood work to be your best friend if they have the slightest inkling that there is money involved.

Needless Guilt Horror

I witnessed this one. Betsy, less than thirty years old, had a daughter age three and a daughter less than one, lost her husband in a farm accident. A tractor rolled over on him, killing him instantly. It was obviously very traumatic to lose a husband completely unexpectedly, at such a young age, with such small children. Betsy had sufficient insurance money, wise counsel about money from her wealthy father, and a home that was paid for.

What she also had was a tremendous amount of guilt over her relationship with her former husband – she felt guilty about, what was in her mind now, a lack of frequency with which they shared intimacy during their marriage. In what was otherwise completely out of character for her, she had empty sexual relationships with at least four men within a year after her husband died. She needlessly encountered multiple horrors in a futile attempt to assuage what was largely false guilt.

Other Horrors

If a woman chooses to engage in a serious relationship, she can gravitate towards what she feels was missing in her prior marriage, what she fears was or will be, or what she feels guilty about from that marriage. This can lead to the following, initially good feeling and lower intensity, but longer lasting, more profound, horrors:

- In her prior marriage she never went to church – remarried a man who was deeply religious and they conflicted over "everything".
- A woman who felt guilty about how much fun she had in her first marriage – married a quiet, reliable, yet overly serious person with whom she shares very limited interests.
- An older woman who feels like she had little fun/all responsibility in her first marriage – gets involved in irresponsible fun as a widow.
- A woman who encountered considerable financial hardship due to her husband's death – overdoes the pursuit of financial security to the detriment of all other aspects of relationship. She now has financial security and little else.

"Friends" or acquaintances who could gain from Sarah's financial situation are going to come out of the wood work. I was told that one banker who never could get out of his chair to speak to one woman while she was married, became so very concerned about her financial well being after he learned that she had just received an $800,000 insurance settlement. You need to get a reputable financial specialist to help Sarah with her investments, taxes, estate and cash flow; in a later chapter I'll show you how to do just that.

Nipping Horror in the Bud

Remembering from the prior chapter on a New Mindset, that a widow feels "numb" or "in a fog", and therefore, it is most reasonable to expect that her equilibrium is, at least somewhat, out of balance. This can affect her perceptions of her relationship with her former husband (I didn't give enough), it can intensify the perception that a rather small issue is much bigger than reality (my life is/was not exciting enough), and it can skew her judgment of people's character, intentions, and integrity (my new best friend is so *helpful* or my lean and tanned golf pro is so *loving*).

You know engaging in relationships or activities that she already knows are harmful and dangerous, only makes the grief, guilt, and trouble worse. But she may not think this way because she has already experienced the most difficult thing she will ever encounter – the loss of her husband. In a perverse way she may rationalize that "I've already been through the worst possible situation, even if I get hurt in this, how bad can it be in comparison?"

All of the women and situations I described above had some deficit that either really did exist (I need financial help) or that they believed existed when it really didn't (I'm bored, I'm guilty). So how does a friend help a friend in this situation?

Telling Jane that her tennis pro isn't good for her won't prevent Jane from making this tremendous mistake, but helping Jane to realize how full and exciting her life is presently (grandkids, friends, travel, freedom, business) and the opportunities that exist before her just might (grandkids, friends, travel, freedom, business). She needs to have someone help her see that even though she is devastated by what has happened (stage 4 of grieving), that this too, in time, will pass.

Telling Betsy to stop sleeping around won't help, but helping Betsy to see she is stuck in stage 3 of the grief process (believing what happened is her fault) may give her the perspective she needs to act more wisely. Ask her what she did that caused his death. Help her to gain an accurate awareness of reality – lack of sex, if there ever was a lack of sex, had nothing to do with a tractor rolling over on top of him. I can imagine that me writing that frankly is startling to you – if it is startling to you, perhaps being that frank is what will bring your Betsy back to reality on this one.

Clearly, all of these women experienced additional threats to their emotional, financial, and sometimes physical sense of security through their actions and decision making. Many did and continue to pay an enormous price. The actions around these horror stories gain a foothold out of the skewed perceptions that come normally when one has experienced serious trauma and change. Using the information in this chapter and in the previous chapter, may help you can gain a basic understanding of where your friend is stuck and how to help her forward.

Chapter 5 - Taxes

"They said I live in a wonderful country
and should pay my taxes with a smile! I
tried that but they insisted on CASH!"
--Mel Narvey

I know of no one who enjoys taxes, as even the CPA's and attorneys I have worked with over the years, have serious questions about the application and administration of most tax programs. Susan is not going to enjoy them either. But armed with some information, the frustration can be minimized, mistakes can be avoided, and that's what I hope this section will do – reduce the frustration and avoid mistakes associated with taxes.

Let's first deal with the taxes that either Susan is most likely to encounter or to have concerns about:

<u>Estate Taxes</u>

Here is a bit of good news. Under current (2009) federal and state law in all states, Susan can completely avoid any and all estate taxes as result of the loss of her husband. Due to what is called the "Unlimited Marital Deduction", Susan can receive from her husband's estate any and all property with no estate or gift tax.

It may not be in her best interests to do so, but she can receive anything from her husband's estate without tax. If the joint estate is over $1 million, it is worth asking an attorney if her husband's assets should be placed in a trust, with Susan as the trustee. Placing assets in trust still allows Susan to receive liberal income from the assets in the broad categories of health, education, maintenance, and support, but it potentially protects these assets from estate tax at her future death as well as protects them from creditors in many, but not all, cases.

Life Insurance Taxes

Proceeds from his life insurance policy paid to Susan or to a trust that Susan benefits from are almost always received income tax free and estate tax free. If her husband owned a business and the insurance proceeds were payable to the company, but intended for Susan, income taxes could come into play depending upon the business structure and business tax status. However, life insurance proceeds payable directly to Susan as beneficiary, or to a trust for Susan's benefit, are not subject to income tax.

Property Taxes

This is an area that is not too terribly complicated, unless a payment is missed. Some states (such as Michigan) require semi-annual property tax payments. Other states (such as Texas) require property taxes on real estate be paid by January 31 of the following year.

If there is a mortgage on Susan's home, her mortgage company is no doubt accruing the property tax payments in an escrow account by requiring a higher monthly mortgage payment. If Susan's home is paid off, property tax valuations and bills should come directly to her address. It is worthwhile to make certain that these notices are arriving in a way that protects her ability to make timely and accurate property tax payments.

Also, check to see if your city, county, municipality, and/or state have exemptions or other tax reductions for widows.

Income Taxes

The Federal Government and most states tax: 1) salary income, 2) dividend and interest income, and investment profits called 3) capital gains. Almost all women in Susan's position will be affected by these taxes.

70

If she works as an employee, she will have income taxes withheld from her salary and/or wages each pay period. The important thing to keep in mind here is to withhold an adequate amount of tax each year, without giving the government an "interest free loan" by having too much withheld. If Susan has children, she should adjust her tax withholding to a status as "head of household" and then add the number of dependents that she has to her withholding status to avoid having too much tax withheld. This is not a perfect solution which will guarantee a refund or no tax due at the end of the year. But it will usually approximate the amount of tax due on her wages.

If Susan has bank accounts, money market accounts, or investment accounts she will have dividend, interest, and capital gain income. Taxes are generally not withheld from the payments she receives from these investments. If interest and dividends make up any meaningful portion of her income, she must file and pay quarterly estimated tax payments to avoid being assessed underpayment penalties when she files her personal income tax return on April 15th. These estimated payments are accomplished on IRS form 1040 ES and information about them is available at http://www.irs.gov/pub/irs-pdf/f1040es.pdf.

There may be a situation in which taxes have already been paid to the IRS on behalf of Susan's husband, where a refund is due to her or to the estate. She must claim any refund on IRS form 1310. Information of doing this is contained at http://www.irs.gov/pub/irs-pdf/f1310.pdf.

A final tax return must be filed for Susan's husband. As his wife, she is likely to have obligations here. If she is also an executor, trustee, or personal representative then she is responsible for the accurate collection of information and the prompt filing of the final tax return. Information about completing this requirement is contained in IRS publication 559 and is available at http://www.irs.gov/pub/irs-pdf/p559.pdf.

Depending upon the state of their residence, a final state income tax return may also be required. Information is usually available by searching Yahoo.com for "New York State Income Tax" or the name of the state in which she lives.

Chapter 6 - Investments

Investing is simple, but not easy.
 --Warren Buffet

Let's begin with a very important distinction – the difference between investing and gambling.

While the odds of gambling successfully, whether in Las Vegas or in the investment markets, are stacked against you, the odds of investing successfully can become almost certain by understanding and applying a few basic guidelines and principals.

Gambling is risking money on the arbitrary outcome or timing of a particular event. "I'm betting $10,000 that the price of this stock will go up within the month irrespective of what the business does". This person may know the name of what they purchased, but they know nothing about the finances of the business, what the company really does, how it makes money, what the likelihood is that the company will continue to make money at its present pace, or what the risks to the business are.

Investing has two possible components. 1) Purchasing a business or piece of property because it will be more valuable in the future and the price will increase as a result, or 2) Loaning money to someone who will pay it back with interest. Investing means knowing the business or the borrower, understanding where the funds are going to come from to pay the investor, what the risks to the payments are, and so forth.

Gambling can be done with little or no forethought, so it can be done quickly, even on the spur of the moment and/or in a rush of emotion. Investing requires time, effort, and expense to thoroughly evaluate and research the business. Good, timely, useful information on the business can be a challenge to find. So given the choice between the two, the quick and easy versus the tough and time consuming, most people *unconsciously* gamble instead of invest - AND THEIR POOR INVESTMENT RESULTS prove the odds are stacked in someone else's favor.

Before we discuss the investment guidelines that will allow you to be successful, first let's talk about a few "investments" you should avoid:

- Friend or Family Loans. If Beverly has recently received an insurance or legal settlement, family members may come to her for a loan to start a business or payoff old debts. DO NOT LOAN the money, even to family members, in this situation. The riskiest investment one can make is in the startup business of someone else. This is why banks generally do not loan money for new businesses – it's *because this type of loan ends up a huge loss so easily and so frequently.* There are groups of people called venture capitalists and angel investors who exclusively make these kinds of investments for a living. If someone has run up a bunch of debts, there are credit counselors and agencies who work out payment plans and renegotiated terms on the balances. Leave the business start up and debt consolidation loans to those folks. If the family member has already tried these avenues and has found no takers, it's a clear indication that Beverly should not risk her funds, when the professionals are unwilling to do so.

- Understand that very few people can successfully invest their own or other people's money. Here is the reason why: To be a successful investor, one must make decisions that are the opposite of what the majority is doing and talking about. Most people take a certain amount of comfort in what others are doing. Acting consistent with the timing and actions of others is an excellent idea when it comes to freeway driving, but it is a ticket to disaster when it comes to investing.

One of the best decisions most people make is finding an investment advisor who can safely produce the results that are needed (see the next chapter for information on finding a great investment advisor).

- In order to produce above average returns with limited risk, you must invest in the right things and do so at the right times. Investing in the *right things at the wrong times* means that your investments go down in value. This was the collateral damage caused by the economic meltdown of 2008. Investing in the *wrong things at any time* can cause all of your investment to evaporate. This was what happened to many people who invested in hedge funds, derivatives, and mortgage loans which caused the economic crisis of 2008.

Investment Overview

In the broadest sense, these are the six things that need to be known or completed for Beverly to have a chance at investing successfully:

- Amount and timing of Beverly's expenses. On an annual basis broken down by month, you need to know the amount of her expenses. How much for utilities, housing, insurance, transportation, taxes, medical, entertainment, and so forth? When, to the best of her knowledge, are these amounts due? What are possible surprise expenses for repairs? What are her medical deductibles and co-pays?

- A plan to produce the cash flow needed to cover expenses. Beverly's investments must produce cash for her on a regular basis so that she has the money to pay her bills. This must be accomplished through some combination of salary/wages, interest, and dividends. Selling investments at the last minute to raise needed cash puts her investments at great risk of loss, so ongoing cash production is essential. Given the current low interest rate environment, it is even more challenging, because the rates paid on interest accounts at the bank are so low.

- A plan to deal with investment risk. Most widows do not have a surplus of funds stashed away somewhere to compensate for any investment mistakes. We define risk as the permanent loss of investment money. Know that any investment, including bank guaranteed investments, will fluctuate in price and/or return over time. This makes a plan to deal with these changes absolutely imperative, so that fluctuations do not turn into permanent losses that cause shortages of cash flow.

- <u>A plan to deal with inflation</u>. In 2000, a gallon of gas cost less than a dollar. In 2009, it costs more than two dollars. Beverly's investments must be able to accommodate this kind of change without increasing risk, or she won't be able to live a stable and normal life.

- <u>A disciplined investment strategy</u>. Beverly must have an approach that will enable her to make the right investments at the right times. This happens only with a sound strategy about *what* to invest in, *when* to invest, *how much* to invest, *how long* to hold, and *when to sell*, redeem, mature, or have paid back.

- <u>Integration between expense, cash flow, risk, inflation, investment strategy and taxes</u>. Some investments, such as retirement accounts, are taxed at ordinary income rates which can be the highest of all tax rates. Some investments are taxed at qualified dividend and capital gain rates which can be lower, depending upon how much ordinary income Beverly has. If she is not at the maximum ordinary income tax rate, a small amount of additional income taxed at ordinary income rates can substantially increase her taxes. All of this is different from person to person. Increased taxes reduce the money Beverly has to spend. Effective tax planning is imperative to making her investment plans succeed for the long term.

Investment Specifics – What Beverly Must Do to Invest her Money Successfully

There are no "new" investments. Every investment from the beginning of time has been one of two things: an ownership interest or a loan. All investments are based on these two things. So in order to successfully manage money, one must make good decisions about what you own and to whom you're willing to loan. Here is the substance of those decisions that are required:

• <u>You must determine which businesses or borrowers will be successful</u>. For an investment to produce the return you need, the underlying business or borrower must work out well. You must determine which ones will fail and avoid them, and which ones will be successful and invest in them.

- You must determine the real worth or value of the business or collateral. When you buy a new car, the price of the car is on the window sticker. This gives you an idea of how much you must pay to acquire that vehicle. But no where on that sticker does it tell you what it cost the car company to build it. What you must pay, the sticker price, is the price of the car. How much it cost to build it, is what the car is worth. What the car is worth is much more difficult, if not impossible, information to come by. Determining the value of the business is also difficult, but what a business is worth determines the success of your investment program, so it is essential information to have.

- Is the business "on sale"? Once the value of the business has been determined, it's pretty easy to compare the value to the price, to decide whether this is a bargain or not. The difficult part is distinguishing between a business that is priced cheap and a business that is going out of business. To make successful investments you must figure out if the business is temporarily cheap (on sale) or on it's way OUT of existence.

- Determine when to invest. Beverly must understand that the timing of the economy, the timing of the investment, and the timing of investment success are

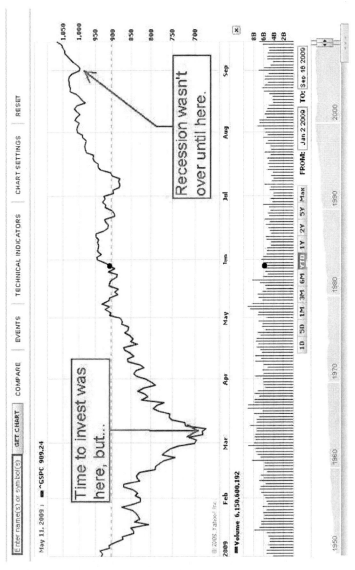

likely to all be different times. This means she must invest at times that may seem counterintuitive (seem wrong). You can see this in the January to September 2009 chart of the S&P 500 index below:

- <u>She must be able to buy when friends, television, radio, newspapers, and so-called-experts all say "sell", and sell when they say "buy"</u>. In March of 2009, all of these sources were telling people to sell, when it is plain from the graph, that the exact opposite was the right thing to do.

- <u>Beverly must be able to live with a certain amount of investment ambiguity and still wait patiently</u> knowing that 1) Investments themselves determine the time of harvest. Imagine that you planted an apple orchard in December and went out to pick an apple in March. Of course this is ridiculous. Everyone knows that apples are harvested in the fall and that it takes 3-5 years before a tree produces any fruit. Investments also have an incubation period. 2) Artificial attempts to minimize ambiguity, force timing, or eliminate natural fluctuations only increase risk and expense. These artificial attempts to bring certainty are going to be proposed in the form of annuities, variable life insurance, equity or index options, derivatives, and so forth. Just remember what Warren Buffett says, "You can't produce a baby in one month by getting nine women pregnant."

* <u>Beverly must produce cash flow from her investments while avoiding losses from selling at the wrong time.</u> Many people invest their funds in such way where when they need cash, they sell an asset. For the many people that did this during 2009, it resulted in permanent investment losses, because as investment prices fell, selling into falling prices meant taking a loss. However, if one had cash being produced, it was possible to wait until investment prices recovered, thus avoiding losses. This is why cash flow must be produced.

* <u>She must coordinate income and the resulting taxes to keep taxes as low as possible.</u> Different investments have different tax requirements. Some investments used to produce cash flow can have the highest tax rates, while others can have very low tax rates. Beverly will need to properly structure and select investments to minimize her taxes.

A Word about "Asset Allocation"

When you hear the words "asset allocation" what comes to your mind is probably the concept of "diversification". First you research a number of investments for quality and expected future results, then you to use an "asset allocation" to "diversify" those investments.

But, when most financial planners say "asset allocation" they mean something entirely different than simple "diversification". What most planners mean is a process of selecting investments where no analysis of the actual investment is done. And one which focuses only on historic asset classes and sectors. (Asset classes meaning large cap funds, small cap funds, mid cap, long term bond, short term bond etc. Sectors being domestic, international, consumer stables, manufacturing, health care, and so forth.) The basic premise of the theory of asset allocation is that it does not matter what specific investments you make, it only matters that you are in the right asset classes and sectors.

Imagine that you had unknowingly invested in the "large cap banking sector" in 2007. You would have owned pieces of Washington Mutual, Wachovia, JP Morgan Chase, and Wells Fargo among others. You probably notice that two of those companies no longer exist and the shareholders of both took a bath (Washington Mutual and

Wachovia). But if in 2007, you invested only in the highest quality banks instead of the entire sector, you would own only JP Morgan and Wells Fargo. What's more you likely would have a profit in these investments today.

The "asset allocation" that a planner/broker does is an almost instantaneous database search (in something like Morningstar) for historical returns and historical standard deviations with little or no regard for what is actually being invested in. Then he "assembles" a portfolio that meets "your risk tolerance and objectives". You can do this yourself on Morningstar in about 5 minutes.

Not only is this the approach of most of the financial planning world, it is also the approach of most mutual funds. The supposed benefit of asset allocation is that using it reduces risk and increases rates of return. We know from the bank example above and from reading investment statements over the last two years that it does not reduce risk – it actually increases risk.

Now Morningstar has done research on the best mutual fund returns in a study called "How the Best Large Cap Managers Rise Above the Rest". What the study revealed is that the best performing fund managers "focus on picking stocks as opposed to making big sector bets". And "overall,

sector selection was less important of a driver than stock selection for these [funds]". While this is not the premise of the article, and it probably can't be because Morningstar's best clients are financial planners, these statements are in the middle of the report for anyone to see.

What this means is that the best performing investment advisors and managers analyze the individual company that they invest in for quality and anticipated investment return while paying little or no attention to asset classes or sectors. Exactly the opposite of what the vast majority of financial planners and funds do. Is it any wonder that investment performance for so many is so poor?!

Comparing the best funds in the Morningstar report that have been managed an amount of time similar to our investment management tenure gives this investment performance data. The Barfield Group performance was not considered or profiled in Morningstar's report as we are a private investment advisor. However, 1) we use a similar investment approach of investment selection in managing portfolios and 2) this is how our results compare to the funds that were profiled.

If all of this seems complicated and difficult, it is. These are also the reasons I said earlier that very few people can manage their own investments successfully. Which means most people, and probably Beverly included, are going to need professional assistance with investment management. In the next chapter, I outline what you need to know to hire the right person to provide this assistance.

Fund Name	Manager Tenure	Cumulative Return
Brandywine Blue	1/10/1991	359%
Jensen	1/3/1993	185%
Selected American	12/1/1994	247%
The Barfield Group	1/1/1995	396%
Davis NY Venture	10/1/1995	144%
Oakmark Select	11/1/1996	236%

Through 9/30/2009

Chapter 7 - Finding a (Great) Financial Advisor

"Don't confuse fame with success - Madonna
is one - Helen Keller is the other."
-- **Erma Bombeck**

There's a lot of confusion in the marketplace about what makes for a great investment advisor. As we discussed in the previous chapter, successful investing is about two essential things; 1) *What* you invest in, and 2) *When* you make the investment. Obviously, when selecting an investment advisor, you're seeking someone who recognizes and can apply what we discussed there. Seems pretty common sense and it is. But investment advice these days has strayed so far from these two common sense principles, that it can be quite difficult and complicated finding the right advisor. The ideas that follow will clear that confusion and enable you to locate the kind of professional advice and guidance Sally needs.

First thing: Registered Investment Advisor

All too often a supposed financial counselor is a salesman in disguise. In fact, the vast majority of financial "experts" are financial salespeople. One woman I interviewed described them as "sharp dressed sharks"! You need a Registered Investment Advisor because this person or firm has the legal obligation to do what is in your best interests. Financial salespeople (stockbrokers, insurance agents, wealth managers, and those with similar titles) have no such obligation. Only a Registered Investment Advisor must do what is in your best interests. You don't want a doctor who cares more about a drug company than you, and you don't want a financial advisor who puts anyone else's interests ahead of your friend's benefit. You can determine whether or not a potential advisor is registered by simply asking to see his/her registration. If someone is truly a Registered Investment Advisor, they will provide you with a copy of their ADV disclosure form very early in the process – it is important to read it.

Second thing: An absence of conflicts

If someone is going to have your best interests as their primary focus, they must have limited areas where the interests between the two of you are in conflict. Any areas that are in conflict must be disclosed. A simple way to determine one of the major conflicts/concerns is to see the following words on letterhead and stationary: "Securities offered through..." and the name of a broker/dealer followed by the words "Member FINRA/SIPC". When you see these words, you need to know that the advisor is earning commissions for selling you investments. Some Registered Investment Advisors are also investment salespeople, earning commissions off of what they recommend – this is a conflict that runs counter to your interests. The best investment advisors will not have this conflict.

Third thing: Incentives (compensation) that align with your interests and objectives

Early in my career in financial services, I worked for two large and well known investment houses. The compensation structure that I was subject to required that I sell financial products which generated commissions for my employer. There was no requirement that my clients make money on their investments AND there was no way to incent me to make them money, nor any way to compensate me if they did. In summary, my incentives and interests, at a minimum, bore no relation to the results, interest, and objectives investors expected, and at worst, ran completely counter to the interests of my clients.

I hated this arrangement. So I worked quickly and diligently to start my own firm, where I could align my interests with those of my clients. Here, very simply, are how interests get aligned: I receive no commissions whatsoever for the investments I make on your behalf. I get a percentage management fee on the assets that I manage. If your account goes up in value, I get a raise. If your account decreases in value, I get a pay reduction. In this way, my interests are aligned with yours.

Use these first three issues to eliminate a large number of people who have no obligation to provide advice that benefits you – then avoid them. Now you're ready to evaluate the remaining advisors for their skills, capabilities, and their judgment under pressure.

<u>Distinguish between a person who *markets* financial management and a one who *provides* financial management</u>

You should pay management fees only to people who actually manage assets. Many financial planners charge an "assets under management" fee but do no actual management of assets. If your advisor recommends mutual funds, annuities, wrap accounts, and professional managers other than themselves, you are dealing with a *marketer* of financial management and not a *provider*. This means that you are paying management fees twice – once to an actual manager (the mutual fund) and then a second time to someone for marketing. This is a needless double expense which reduces your rate of return. Pay management fees only to people/firms who actually manage your assets.

A great way to tell if you have a marketer or an actual service provider is whether or not you've been told "no". A professional investment advisor gets paid to say no at appropriate times. A professional marketer gets paid to say "yes" all the time. Professional Financial Advisors have produced results for clients even in the recent difficult environment – marketers of financial services have not. Professional advisors offer a simple and fully disclosed breakdown of costs you pay. Marketers seek to obscure their costs by complicated prospectus or long disclosures.

<u>You need someone who addresses a weakness you have, instead of denying or exploiting a weakness you have</u>

You are seeking investment advice because you think and believe that you need assistance. A truly excellent financial advisor produces realistic results over long periods of time that beat the market average called the S & P 500.

An exploiter sees you as a means to increased income. The best way to evaluate this is really very simple. Is there a consistent effort to mask the service offering and service results with "relationship"? A marketer focuses on relationship. An excellent advisor is going to communicate with you primarily about your financial results. Is the substance of your communication about financial issues and concerns? Does the advisor send out expensive gifts to clients? Are you invited to wine and cheese tasting (or the equivalent)? Where do you think the money comes from to do these non-financial related types of things? If you said, from fees, expenses, and charges that you've paid which reduce your investment performance, you would be entirely correct. When was the last time your professional physician sent you an expensive gift? Invited you to a business related wine tasting? Professional financial advisors focus and provide expert advice about your financial matters with your best interest foremost in mind.

Experience and track record

You want someone who has been through difficult periods of time managing your money because they have lived through the trouble and (hopefully) learned from it.

Select someone who has been managing money for at least 15 or 20 years. This means that they have experienced October 1987, worked through the difficult market in the mid-1990's, the Tech Bubble of 2000, the Real Estate Bubble in 2005, and the Sub-Prime meltdown that followed. Ask how they fared in these periods. You want someone who can demonstrate actual account results to go with the published rates of return they provide. This is easy to evaluate by asking for redacted records that show beginning and period ending balances of actual accounts.

You want someone who has outperformed the S & P 500 index through an entire market cycle – this is generally a ten year period or more. A significant majority of investment advisors, quoted frequently as in excess of 90%, fail to outperform this index. If an advisor isn't doing so, you don't want him.

NEVER, EVER put assets in the name of the advisor, ALWAYS keep them in your name

Bernard Madoff was able to steal billions of dollars from people who violated this principle. Always keep the money in your own name at a reliable independent custodian.

In summary, you've found the right (a great) investment advisor when you make sure that he/she:

- Is a Registered Investment Advisor,
- Earns no commissions from the investments recommended to you,
- Has experienced the market difficulties of previous years,
- Uses "asset allocation" as a process of diversification only and not a means to selected investments,
- Has a quantifiable track record,
- Is someone who provides actual investment management instead of someone who markets investment management, and
- Is someone who chooses to serve your interests.

Follow these rules and eliminate most, if not all, of the possible mistakes in choosing an advisor.

Chapter 8 - Health Insurance

The laws of probability, so true in
general, are so fallacious in particular.
--Edward Gibbon

No doubt in losing her husband, Diane has had some
interaction with the medical system. She probably already
has or soon will encounter some idea of the costs of
getting sick. This will concern her, especially if her health
insurance was one of the benefits she received from her
husband's employment.

Let's talk about how to address securing health insurance
for her in a number of different situations. (After
determining the options for Diane's situation in the next
pages, please also see "Ways to reduce health insurance
costs" at the end of this chapter).

**Diane has been getting health insurance through *her*
employer**.

This makes things pretty simple. If she is already
getting/purchasing health insurance through *her* employer,
then she needs to do nothing to continue it. If the rest of
the family was also getting insurance through her

employer, she needs to report the death of her husband to the insurance company directly or through communication to the employer human resources department. If Diane is removing her husband from coverage, she needs to make certain that the billing amount for the insurance is reduced.

Diane has been getting health insurance through her *husband's* employer.

Diane can keep the coverage she has from her husband's employer under a 1986 law known as COBRA[5]. In the case of an employee's death, surviving family members who were on the deceased's health insurance can continue coverage for 36 months after his passing.

His employer can charge her for the coverage at the actual cost plus a two percent administrative charge, but the plan remains the same. What her husband paid for health insurance coverage during his lifetime may have been subsidized by the employer. Under COBRA this employer subsidy is likely to go away, which can result in meaningful increases in the COBRA premiums over what were the

---

[5] COBRA coverage must be offered only by employers who have more than 20 employees. Also churches and certain church related organizations are exempt from offering COBRA.

employee premiums. We have seen employee family premiums increase from $800 per month to $1,500 per month under COBRA.

For the first few months, COBRA coverage is the simplest way for Diane to have health insurance. But as described, it can be expensive. Depending on her health, she may be able to reduce the costs of health insurance by getting quotes from other health insurance companies. The easiest way to do this is on-line at Insure.com. Enter some basic information and the site will direct to potential sources for health insurance. Understand that depending on her health she may or may not qualify, she may or may not have to answer pretty detailed questioning, and she may or may not be required to take a physical.

Diane's employer offers health insurance but up to now she has been getting it through her husband's employer.

Because the death of Diane's husband qualifies as a "Life Change Event" she can sign up for health insurance coverage through her employer now, or she can keep the coverage she has from her husband's employer through COBRA.

COBRA allows Diane to remain on her husband's insurance for up to 36 months after his death. His employer can charge her for the coverage at the actual cost plus a two percent administrative charge, but the plan remains the same.

Keep in mind that what her husband paid for health insurance coverage during his lifetime may have been subsidized by the employer. Under COBRA this employer subsidy is likely to go away, which can result in meaningful increases in the COBRA premiums over what were the employee premiums.

If Diane can get health insurance coverage through her own employer, it is likely the costs will be less than COBRA coverage. If the costs for health insurance are more expensive at her employer than the COBRA from his employer, she can pay for the COBRA for 36 months and at the end of that period, enroll in the insurance at her employer (Loss of COBRA coverage is also considered a "Life Change Event".

<u>Diane has not had health insurance coverage, but now wants it.</u>

Depending on her health, she can probably get health insurance by getting quotes from health insurance companies. The easiest way to do this is on-line at Insure.com. Enter some basic information and the site will direct to potential sources for health coverage. Understand that depending on her health, she may or may not qualify, she may or may not have to answer pretty detailed questioning, and she may or may not be required to take a physical. Be aware the premiums can vary depending on insurance company and the state of Diane's health.

Ways to reduce Diane's health insurance costs

The dollar amounts of deductible and co-pay arrangements are significant factors in determining the cost of health insurance. A plan deductible of $5,000 will result in a significant premium reduction when compared to a plan that has a $500 or a $1,000 deductible. A plan that has a co-pay of $20 for doctor's office visits will be significantly more expensive than a plan where doctor visits must be paid out of pocket until the deductible is met.

For many people in Diane's position, this has never been a concern of theirs because their employer has paid the larger portion of health insurance costs. In this case, a low deductible or generous co-pay arrangement seems most desirable.

But when Diane must pay for coverage on her own, these questions are worth examining (pardon the pun). What if a low deductible plan is going to cost Diane $1,500 per month under COBRA, and a $5,000 deductible plan is going to cost $350 per month direct with an insurance company? The COBRA coverage guarantees that she will spend a minimum of $18,000 per year (12 times $1,500) for health coverage even if she never sits a foot in a doctor's office. With the high deductible plan if she never sets foot in the doctor's office her annual costs are $4,200 – an annual savings of almost $14,000. To have the same out of pocket costs each year as the COBRA (or a low deductible) plan, three different members of the family must max out their deductible. So, if Diane is capable of budgeting her money effectively, she can save thousands of dollars every year, by having a high deductible plan with no (or only a few) co-pays.

Remember that the concept of insurance is to prevent one from going to the "poor house" over a catastrophic event. However, one can buy coverage that eliminates most any and all out-of-pocket costs. But when this latter coverage is chosen, the costs rise quickly and significantly.

For more details on COBRA see

http://www.dol.gov/ebsa/pdf/cobraemployee.pdf.

Sust🔒ined Security

Dear Reader,

There is additional, updated information at our two blog sites.

www.retirementwhys.blogspot.com
www.sustainedsecurity.com

Please subscribe at each site, so that you automatically receive the most recent articles as soon as they are published.

You can also send your e-mail address to free@sustainedsecurity.com and we will send you any of the resources we have available that are mentioned in **Chapter 13: Resources**

We are here to help with your complex issues and asset based income/money management needs. To **ask a question, or schedule a visit in confidence**, call 972-231-4444 or e-mail dana@thebarfieldgroup.com.

With kindest regards,

Dana Barfield

Chapter 9 - Do These Things The First Week

Depending on funeral arrangements, many of the following items can and should be addressed in the time leading up to the funeral. (*There is a checklist for you to work from in "Resources" Chapter 13*)

1. Does Mary have small children? Are they being cared for?
    a. Is there an attempt to reestablish a "normal" routine for them?
    b. Are the kids getting to bed on time and getting sufficient rest?
    c. Are they eating? Are they eating reasonably healthy meals?
    d. Are they beginning to talk about the absence of their dad (even if done so with great emotion)?

2. Are the family bills current?
    a. Where are the bills kept?
    b. When are the next bills due?
    c. Are there sufficient funds in checking accounts to pay them?

d. What will be Mary's source(s) of income? Will this income cover her bills?

e. Does Mary want assistance dealing with the bills? Remember that Mary has a hard time concentrating – this makes bill paying difficult.

f. Are there any bills paid electronically?

g. Are bills paid electronically paid automatically?

h. Are bills paid electronically drawn on an account that is interrupted due to the husband's death?

Please understand that with the following contact items, the companies contacted are likely to require that they speak with the owner of the account or the beneficiary of the policy. In many cases this means they will need to talk with Mary. In some cases, after the initial identification, she can designate someone to speak on her behalf to collect information and request forms. Be prepared for this situation so that neither of you become frustrated by it. Work through it a smoothly as possible.

3. Is there a reason to contact an attorney over the cause of death?

a. Was the situation the result of someone else's reckless or negligent behavior?

b. Did this happen as the result of irresponsibility on the part of an employer?

c.   Was there serious error(s) in the medical treatment he received?

If any of these things took place, contact your family attorney to see what he/she recommends as a course of action. Further, if there is any potential case against someone else, do not sign any final settlements until you have been able to speak with a credible attorney.

Recognize, that even in the case where there may be a reason to pursue legal action Mary may prefer to simply "move on with her life". We have worked with women who had legitimate claims and reasons to seek legal remedy, but they determined that the amount of time and hassle was not something they wanted to deal with. They really preferred to just move on.

Not everyone is going to think the same way. In most every death, there is some lawyer out there who is willing to pursue a claim regardless of how silly it may be. Get trusted counsel on this before you rule out legal action and before you engage an attorney to commence action.

4.   Is there any life insurance that the couple has purchased on the husband?

a. If needed due to expenses, will the life insurance company provide a partial payment to offset short term or unforeseen expenses?

b. Is there any life insurance through his employment?

c. Is there any life insurance from credit card membership?

d. Is there any life insurance due to the cause of death (as the result of an accident on a public mode of transportation)?

e. Is there life insurance through a club membership?

f. Have you been able to locate all of the policies and contact phone numbers?

g. Call each insurance company directly and ask for policy holder service to find out the requirements for filing a claim. Request that they send any needed forms.

h. Even if there is an insurance agent, I recommend that you call the insurance company direct to reduce delays and facilitate the prompt processing and payment of the claim.

Most insurance companies have a customer service department setup to handle the kind of request that you are going to make. If you have an agent, he/she will be calling the same folks, asking the same questions, and requiring the same paper work. Frequently the agent can't request what is needed without the beneficiary anyway. Contact the insurance company directly.

5. Is there a will and/or trust and have you located the documents? (This is especially important for estates above $1 Million dollars.)
    a. Do the documents call for trusts to be created now?
    b. Are there specific actions mentioned in the documents that must be taken?
    c. Who is the executor and/or trustee? Should these people be notified immediately?

6. Is there a safe deposit box with items in it that should be retrieved right away?

7. Did the man have a personal or family attorney that should be contacted?

8. Did the man own a business? Determine a contact whether partner, attorney, banker, or someone else.

9. Notify the husband's employer of the situation and request any pay for work already completed, vacation time, personal time and so forth.

10. Contact the county where death occurred and find out what is required to obtain death certificates. Acquire copies equal to the number of employers, insurance companies, banks, and investment houses involved and then add five to it.

11. Was the husband a veteran? If so, contact the local Veterans Affairs office for any benefits due or go to www.va.gov and click on "Benefits".

12. Contact the Social Security Administration to notify them of the passing and see what, if any benefits are payable www.ssa.gov/pgm/links_survivor.htm

13. If the husband died while working for his employer, contact the Employer Human Resources department for benefits that are due as a result. *Ask about health insurance status*.

14. Contact present or former employers to determine what vested and/or survivor benefits are paid from husband's pension plan(s).

15. Contact present or former employers to determine what options are available for account balances in 401(k) plans.

16. Are there arrangements that need to be made for yard work or regular maintenance?

Chapter 10 - Do These Things The First Month

These things need to be addressed in most cases, beginning a week or so after the funeral. Having said that I am mindful of the recent situation of Michael Jackson, whose funeral took place weeks after his passing, and at the time of this writing (almost two months after his death) he has still not been laid in a final resting place.

For most people, the funeral and services associated with it will be completed within a week's time. In a case such as this, I suggest that you give Jill another week to adjust and develop a routine, then begin addressing this set of concerns and issues in week three or four of the first month.

1. Are there any medical or other end-of-life expenses that need to be paid out of pocket and what provision has been made for these?

Understand that many hospital expenses are marked up significantly. Seek to negotiate the final payment in light of the circumstances.

The following items should be done taking into consideration the instructions contained in his will and/or trust documents, and probably with the assistance of the family attorney:

2. Determine if there is a will that must be probated.

Even if Jill's husband had a living trust, it is possible that there are assets that will transfer by will. Determine if this is the case or not.

3. Change the titling on any individual bank or investment accounts Jill's husband may have had. In most states and circumstances this gets changed from individual name to "Estate of John Doe". (You will need a copy of the death certificate to do this.)

4. Change the titling on any joint bank or investment accounts Jill's husband may have had.

5. Change any automobile titles by contacting the Department of Motor Vehicles or the Secretary of State.

6. Remove Jill's husband from the car insurance billing. This should reduce the cost of this insurance going forward.

7. Analyze health insurance options and decide what health insurance to carry going forward. If they are paying for health or health related insurance of some kind, remove deceased from this billing and seek refund for any "unearned premiums".

Unearned premiums are amounts which have been paid to the insurance company, but because coverage ceased after his death, were not due to the insurance company. Obviously at the time the premium payments were made this was not known. A refund should be requested for these unearned premiums whether medical, car, life or disability insurance.

8. Get any insurance checks deposited into a money market account.

Be aware that financial people are going to "come out of the woodwork" as one woman put it. Jill may be invited to "special presentations" with our "team of experts". She may be seduced by "better rates" and provisions than normal. Keep a level head about all this.

If the beneficiary of the insurance was a trust, be certain to open the money market account in the trust name to preserve the benefits of the trust for Jill. It may be that the trust provides protection against creditors or some sort of tax advantage. Be careful to identify provisions, establish accounts, and then deposit insurance proceeds according to these details.

Depending upon Jill's tax situation and net worth, a non-FDIC insured account may pay greater interest with fewer taxes. It may also be wise to place this money into a trust, LLC or other creditor protected instrument. These things are more likely to be needed the greater income and net worth Jill will have going forward.

Remember also that an insurance check is likely to be the single largest transaction Jill has ever done and will ever do. Don't be in a hurry to determine how it should be invested, but don't dawdle either. Until Jill has had a conversation with a qualified financial specialist in this area, do not loan money to friends or family members, as she may not be able to afford it. To many, when a woman receives a check for several hundred thousand or even a million dollars, they may think, "What do you mean she may not able to afford it??!!" Just remember, in this present low interest rate environment, three percent of even a million dollars is still only $30,000 of annual income. This amount of income when considering recent inflation does not make one rich at all. Don't make loans or other financial decisions until expert help has been consulted!

9. Assemble all credit card information. Determine if there are cards that should be cancelled, have the name change or be otherwise altered.

Multiple factors come into play here. Past needs that have changed, future needs that aren't fully known yet, and affects to credit rating and scoring are just a couple that need to be considered.

10. Plan a budget for monthly and annual expenses. (*A budget worksheet is available at our website*).

If her house is paid off, then property taxes need to be paid annually in most states and semiannual in others. Make sure to include these amounts for monthly saving even though they occur less frequently than monthly.

Determine the payment schedule for house and car insurance. Some people pay these premiums semi-annually or annually if there is a cost savings to be achieved or simply to avoid writing monthly checks. Be sure to include these items in the monthly budget.

Make certain that if Jill will owe income tax for this year, that estimated tax payments are made quarterly to avoid underpayment penalties with the IRS. This is accomplished on form 1040ES. Information is at http://www.irs.gov/pub/irs-pdf/f1040es.pdf.

Depending on the time of year that Jill's husband passed, he may be due a tax refund that should now be paid to Jill or the estate. This is accomplished on form 1310. For more information on this, go to http://www.irs.gov/pub/irs-pdf/f1310.pdf.

Here is the IRS information for survivors, executors and personal representatives regarding filing the final tax return for Jill's husband. This is publication 559 and it can be accessed at: http://www.irs.gov/pub/irs-pdf/p559.pdf.

Chapter 11 - Do These Things The Second Month

1. Seek the advice of a professional financial advisor who at a minimum has *significant experience in producing asset-based income*. (***Who is a professional financial advisor and how to recognize him/her is discussed in Chapter 7***).

    a. Even if she ran the money perfectly while her husband was alive, generating income from investments and dealing with taxes are complex issues. She will need help.

    b. Understand that Debra is not in any position to survive a mistake when it comes to financial advice. Make sure that you distinguish between a financial salesman and someone who offers true expert, financial counsel. Financial salesmen rely primarily on relationship in dealing with their customers. They do this because they lack true expertise in financial matters. Believe me, if Debra's husband was sick for a while, they did everything they could to find the best qualified surgeons, anesthesiologists, and nurses to solve their problem. A fine bedside manner was important, but skill in removing tumors, administering medications, and inserting IVs was much more important. A good professional advisor will also have a decent "bedside manner", but more importantly he/she will have expertise in solving Debra's concerns and accomplishing Debra's objectives.

c. A whole host of new people now offer "financial services" – from your good neighbor insurance agent to the person that used to loan money at the local bank. Understand that the person who writes the insurance on your home and car specializes in insuring homes and cars. The financial advice that they offer is limited to selling insurance-related investment products – not in producing a secure and sustainable income for a woman who recently lost her husband. *Their training, their approach, their systems, and their service are all designed to sell financial products, not offer expert financial advice.* Further, even though the training that homeowners insurance agents have received may be the best in the world, they have limited or no experience in dealing with the realities of complex finances. I have been with the same auto and home insurance company for 18 years and I am extremely pleased with how they have treated me. But I see what they send me to offer financial advice and I have seen what they recommend to those they "advise" - this is not what Debra needs.

d. Banks used to have trust departments – they were trustable in most cases but very expensive to deal with. Only a few banks have them any more. Banks now have "wealth management" departments. Like the neighborhood insurance agents, banks saw what they believe to be lucrative fees from giving advice and managing other people's money. Also like the insurance agents, they have limited expertise in actually managing people's money, so they hire outside managers to manage the funds. If this seems complicated, even convoluted, it is. What ends up happening is that a client, like Debra, ends up paying the bank or the insurance company an increased fee, so that they can be paid to sell the management of another company, that Debra could have hired on her own to begin with. All this comes with promises of guarantees and wonderful rates of return. What really happens is that Debra ends up with high expenses for multiple firms to have their hands in,

which reduces her return and the income available
to her to meet her expenses.

e.   Large investment houses do expensive television
commercials and sponsor golf tournaments. They
wax on eloquently about their "global reach" or
"years of experience" or their "concern for their
relationship with you." Every one of these
companies is a conduit for financial sales of
products they produce. They are not financial
experts offering good advice to your best interests.
In fact, financial regulation does not require that
insurance agents, wealth managers, and
stockbrokers have their client's best interests at
heart. Only a registered investment advisor is
required by law to do what is in the best interests of
his clients at all times.

f.   Do not assume that the financial guy that you go to
church with is the right person to deal with. (***Read
Chapter 7 carefully to know how to choose the
right professional financial advisor.***)

2.   Debra needs to review her wills, trusts and estate
plans.

This is especially the case if she has children she is supporting who have not yet completed college. If she has minor children, she may need to name new guardians for her kids in the event of her absence. She may need to establish medical powers of attorney in the event she requires serious medical attention and is unable to make her own decisions. She may need a new will because her husband can no longer be her executor and/or trustee. As the head of the household now, these things are critical to protect herself and her dependents.

3. Do a life insurance evaluation on Debra's life insurance.

Again, as head of the household, there may be financial risk to her absence. If she has significant debt this is also the case.

4. **DO NOT**, in an effort to simplify things, **combine any IRA accounts, pension accounts, 401(k) accounts** and so forth. Don't combine the same types of accounts and don't combine different types of accounts into one either. There are potential serious tax consequences that are detrimental to Debra if this is done improperly.

Chapter 12 - Do These Things The Third & Fourth Month

1. As account statements, billings or other communications are received, make certain that name changes, billing amounts, and any other requested changes have taken place and are accurate.

2. Under normal circumstances, insurance claims should have been processed and checks received by this time. Check to make certain that this has taken place.

3. Evaluate the accuracy of the budget that was established.
    a. Are expenses getting paid on time?
    b. Are there budget amounts or assumptions that are off and need to be adjusted?
    c. Are electronic payments processing properly?

4. If Karen has children who are minors, follow up with teachers to make sure her kids are dealing with their loss in appropriate and healthy ways.

5. How is Karen dealing with her loss?
    a. Is she still in denial?

b. Is she overly discouraged or depressed?

c. Has she come to some sense of acceptance?

6. Now is a probably good time to invite Karen to a new activity or event. She is not interested yet in something that looks and/or feels like a date – so don't go there, but seek to engage her in something that fits her personality and interests.

7. Recognize now that the activities, well wishers, and to-dos have begun to subside, the loneliness will begin to set in for Karen. Quiet encouragements along with listening, and words of affirmation, are very helpful here.

8. If Karen has made even modest progress, praise her for it.

If she has shown strength in the face of difficulty, tell her so. If she has been able to reestablish a sense of order and process, acknowledge it. Go back to the basic mindset for Karen's personality type in the chapter on Grieving and compliment her consistent with the traits and strengths of the otter, retriever, beaver, or lion.

Chapter 13 - Resources

If you'll send us an e-mail, we'll send you these available resources. (We never sell or share your information.)

- First Week Checklist
- First Month Checklist
- Second Month Checklist
- Three/Four Month Checklist
- Beneficiary Checklist
- Executor Checklist
- Budget worksheets

On our website www.sustainedsecurity.com you'll find this additional information:

- Estimated Income Tax Payments Data

- Deceased Income Tax Refund Data

- Final Tax Return filing information

- Social Security web site

- COBRA Health Insurance details from Department of Labor

- Veterans Affairs office web site

- Web address for Secretary of State for each state.

- Common life insurance company 800 numbers and web sites

Sust🔒ined Security

Dear Reader,

There is additional, updated information at our two blog sites.

www.retirementwhys.blogspot.com
www.sustainedsecurity.com

Please subscribe at each site, so that you automatically receive the most recent articles as soon as they are published.

You can also send your e-mail address to free@sustainedsecurity.com and we will send you any of the resources we have available that are mentioned in **Chapter 13: Resources**

We are here to help with your complex issues and asset based income/money management needs. To **ask a question, or schedule a visit in confidence**, call 972-231-4444 or e-mail dana@thebarfieldgroup.com.

With kindest regards,

Dana Barfield

dividends, 37, 41
dumbness, 17

E

eating, 16, 54
employer, 47, 50, 51, 52, 54, 55
equilibrium, 26, 34
Estate Taxes, 36
estimated tax payments, 37, 57
executor, 38, 55, 59
expenses, 11, 40, 41, 48, 55, 56, 57, 58, 60

F

family, 9, 12, 13, 15, 39, 50, 52, 54, 55, 56, 57
Family Loans, 39
fears, 15, 33
finances, 4, 12, 14, 16, 39, 58
focus, 16, 25, 26, 28, 45, 46, 48
fog, 17, 18, 34
forgiveness, 20, 21
fraud, 12
friends, 4, 5, 32, 35, 43, 57
frustration, 15, 36
fully disclosed, 48
fun, 22, 23, 24, 27, 34

G

gambling, 39
God, 5, 15, 16, 18, 21

grieve, 10, 15, 22, 24, 25, 29, 30
grieving, 10, 16, 18, 19, 20, 21, 22, 23, 24, 26, 27, 29, 30, 35
Grieving, 19, 22, 29, 60
grieving process, 16, 20, 27
guilt, 24, 33, 34

H

harvest, 43
health, 36, 44, 50, 51, 52, 55, 56
Health Insurance, 8, 50, 61
healthy way, 15, 17, 22, 27
higher power, 21
honest, 13, 16
hope, 20, 36
horror, 32, 33, 35

I

in her shoes, 14
income, 9, 12, 36, 37, 38, 41, 44, 48, 53, 54, 57, 58, 61
Income Taxes, 37
inflation, 41, 57
insurance, 9, 10, 11, 23, 33, 34, 36, 39, 40, 43, 46, 50, 51, 52, 54, 55, 56, 57, 58, 59, 60, 61
insurance company, 50, 52, 55, 56, 58

Breinigsville, PA USA
21 December 2010
251958BV00001B/50/P